ON THE OTHER
SIDE OF FAITH

Where Faith meets Foolishness

Savannah
Everett

PROMINENT
BOOKS
EDGE

5830 E 2nd St, Ste 7000 #9983
Casper, WY 82609
USA

Table of Contents

Introduction

This book gives readers a practical view on how to use their faith to obtain the promises of God. There seems to be a lot of confusion concerning matters of faith, especially when it deals with giving money or sowing financial seeds. This book gives clarity on faith and giving while utilizing a straightforward approach. After reading this book one should have a better understanding of what faith is and how to realistically apply faith in everyday life situations.

Chapter 1

What is Faith?

Faith, according to the dictionary it is defined as firm belief in something for which there is no proof of the intended outcome, only complete trust. What does it mean to place total confidence in someone or something?

There is much debate concerning the existence of God. People feel the wind and they know it's there as it can only be felt. It is the same way with God. He exists; however you may not see Him. He can be felt and seen in others only if you will take a closer, more in-depth look.

According to the Message bible, Hebrews 11:1 says faith is, "The fundamental fact of existence is that this trust in God, this faith, is the firm foundation under everything that makes life worth living. It's our handle on what we can't see. The act of faith is what distinguished our ancestors, set them above the crowd."

The Amplified bible says in Hebrews 11:1, "Now faith is the assurance (the confirmation, the title deed) of the things [we] hope for, being the proof of things [we] do not see *and* the conviction of their reality [faith perceiving as real fact what is not revealed to the senses]."

Faith is acting as if I already have it when the thing that I am believing for is not yet in the natural realm. Such belief has manifested in the realm of the spirit. As a result, I see myself healed, prosperous, debt free, and wealthy, amongst other goals and ambitions.

My faith says, "I already have it before I can touch, taste, or smell it." Let me be clear, I am not suggesting that if you need a job that you are to stay home and pray all day without doing the work. The bible also says that, "faith without works is dead". James 2:17 KJV(paraphrase). You are to pray and ask God for employment, get out of your own way, and then follow His leading. He will lead you to the right people, places, and even resources, and when you arrive, the favor is already there. The situation that you are involved in, the circumstance in which you must activate your faith may get worse. Just know that this is a clear indication that your faith is indeed activated.

Stop being your own compass! Allow God to lead and direct you! Your five senses can perhaps land you in a world of trouble when it comes to using your faith. The five senses can also cause you to doubt the very thing you are believing God for. The bible says that "a man that waivers gets nothing from God, he like the waves of the sea." James 1:6 (KJV)

You must remain stable and firm in your faith. There have been times when things were manifested. But from a personal point of view, I did not stay fixed in faith to maintain my blessing. I purchased a car without a verifiable income. I received what I thought was a blessing. However, how is it a blessing when I was jumping from job to job and did not have stable income to make my payments? To make a long story short I had to file bankruptcy and give the car back. The reason being was that my payment was over $400.00 a month for a Chevy Cavalier.

Looking back on it now, this scenario does not even make sense. At the time, I said to myself, "I am stepping out on faith."

As human beings, many would argue that God has given us common sense, and we need to use it. On the other hand, the ways of God are oftentimes illogical. However, the Word of God says, "Let all things be done decently and in order. Did my purchasing a car without a steady job and having to file bankruptcy go against the order of God? The bible also says, "Money answereth all things." The scripture also states to seek first the kingdom of God, and all these things will be added unto you." Did I desire a car (a material possession) more than waiting on God or going about things the correct way? Or was this faith or an act of stupidity?

Chapter 2

Who Has Faith?

Everyone has faith. Everyone has complete trust and reliance on someone or something. It could be total faith and reliance on a spouse, job, money, car, etc. If your faith is in those people or things, then you will surely be disappointed. I must advise you that your faith is misplaced. God never fails or disappoints His children. He may not work things out the way that we thought He would. Nevertheless, He always works things out. Not only does He work things out, but He works them out for our good. It could be the most devastating situation in your life. God has a way turning negative things into something positive. My young nephew was tragically killed in a car accident back in 2016. It was totally unexpected and completely devastating. My family misses him terribly and so do I. One thing that I've gained from his passing is to cherish every moment with the ones you love. Make time for them. Tomorrow is not promised, and you must make the best out of every day.

Tell the people in your life that are important that you love them and mean it. Give people their flowers while they can still smell them. Offer words of encouragement while the person can hear them.

The bible says in Romans 12:3B (Amplified Bible), "God has apportioned to each a degree **of faith** [and a purpose designed for service]." God has given each of us a measure of faith to be used to trust Him in our lives. Some people have great faith while others possess little confidence in our Lord.

Only God knows whether a person has great or little faith. Many people can trust God when things are going north. But can you trust God when things are going south?

Can you trust God when all hell breaks loose in your life? Can you trust the Creator to know that He has a plan for your life? In the event you do not understand the plan will you still follow Him and remain in faith knowing that it will work for your good because you love Him? Romans 8:28 says, "All things work together for good to them that love the Lord and are called according to his purpose." (KJV)

The Amplified bible states Romans 8:28 like this, "And we know [with great confidence] that God [who is deeply concerned about us] causes **all things** to **work together** [as a plan] for good for those who love God, to those who are called according to His plan *and* purpose." The Amplified version of scripture confirms that God has a plan and a purpose for our lives. Also, God is greatly concerned about us.

Psalms 126:5 King James Version says, "They that sow in tears will reap in joy." Walking the Christian Walk wholeheartedly can be extremely challenging at times.

Those that you thought would always be there for you will turn their back on you and exit out of your life. Even families that have been closely knit will turn against you. I once was a member of a certain church. During my time there I remember how one of the members had stated that their family disowned them because they grew up Catholic. As a result, such spiritual conflict led to this church member transitioning to the apostolic faith.

Chapter 3

What Does Faith Look Like?

Since faith deals with the unseen and unfelt the only way I know how to illustrate what faith looks like is to go to the passage of scripture that deals with Peter walking on the water. Matthew 14:22-33 explains how Jesus gave his disciples instruction to get on a boat and go to Galilee. The winds and the waves tossed and shook the boat. During the storm the disciples see a figure walking on the water and say to themselves, "Is it a ghost?"

Peter says, "Lord if it is you bid me come?" As a result, it was Jesus. Peter steps out of the boat and begins to walk on water. From scripture, we know that while Peter kept his eyes on Jesus, he did not sink which means he was safe. On the contrary however the moment the disciple shifted his eyes from Jesus he began to sink. Peter then cried out, "Help Lord!" Jesus came to his rescue, and he was saved. If Jesus is bidding, you to take a step of faith in areas of your life then be not doubtful because our Lord is obligated to see you through. You must know his voice and that he is beckoning you to walk on the water as well as entering areas that are unchartered for you. The word of God says, "My sheep hear my voice, and I know them, and they follow me..." John 10:27 (KVJ). The only way to know God's voice is to spend time with him. This is through praying, reading your bible, fasting, and worshiping him. To have a relationship with someone you spend time with them. Many of us are spending time with everybody else, but God. Then you wonder why you are making the wrong moves.

Spending time alone with Jesus will allow you to maneuver over, past, and proceed victoriously through the snares of the devil.

There are individuals in your life that are sent to set you up to fall and to fail. Spending time alone with Jesus allows you to defeat the plans of the enemy everything time. If you miss the mark and it turns out you did not hear from God, pick yourself up, repent, and start over. When you pick yourself up the objective is to learn from your mistakes. Stop making the same mistakes repeatedly with a mindset that things will be different this time, because it won't.

Faith is being a good steward over the God's blessings. If he has blessed you with a new or newer car, or house, you should not let them fall apart but rather take care of them. The car is to stay washed as well as routine maintenance. Concerning the house, you do not let it fall apart by not fixing the roof or not performing maintenance on the water heater, air conditioning, furnace, etc. We are to take care of our blessings but at the same time we are not to make gods out of our possessions. You maintenance your belongings with care so God can be proud that he gave them to you and not be sorrowful that he blessed you.

As you wait on your blessing(s), you
trust and thank God that it is coming.
You should not get jealous and envious
of your brother or sister in Christ. This
could be a test to see if you are ready

for your blessing(s). Should you display jealousy then obviously you are not ready to be blessed. The Word of God says, "Rejoice with them that rejoice, mourn with them that mourn."

Romans 12:15 (KJV).

Chapter 4

Faith versus Deception

Faith is not being self-deceived. Deception is running rampant in the land. The dictionary describes deception as the act of causing someone to accept as true or valid what is false or invalid.

Many times, we can trick ourselves into believing something that is not true. If I am a believer of Jesus Christ, then my bible is the final authority over any situation. There are individuals that lie so much that they eventually believe the lies they tell as truth. We live in a day and age when people call right wrong and wrong right.

The bible says in the King James version God has turned man's wisdom backwards. This means that man's wisdom is foolishness to God. What would seem like the right thing to do man does the opposite and goes in the opposite direction. This is why God says, "In all thy ways acknowledge him and he will direct thy path." Proverbs 3:5 (KJV) the opposite way. We can get so far off the path that God has for us because we choose to go our own way. This is not a popular path, and it is not a broad path. The way is narrow. It is a path to eternal life. The world has gone mad. There are no morals anymore or respect. Women will do anything to get and keep a man. When you have faith and walk this path there are many days you will walk alone. If you are on God's side, you are never alone. People may look at you strange; it is your faith in God that keeps you strong and from being self-deceived. When you know the truth for yourself and really discern whether something is truly of God, he will show you if you want to know the pure unadulterated truth, not the truth that has been diluted with wickedness. That kind of truth is really a lie. The bible says, "A little leaven leaveneth the whole loaf." Galatians 5:9 (KJV)

It's like being a little pregnant, a little drunk, or a little high. The saying goes if it walks like a duck, quacks like a duck, then it's a duck. You can put that duck in a bow tie and suit, and it will still be a duck. The duck can even go play in the mud and again, it will still be a duck. The bible says in Matthew 8:32, "You shall know the truth and the truth shall make you free." You can dress a lie up and put it in a neat little package. No matter how you present it, lies will always be present. A lie has a little truth in it but it will continue to be a lie. The truth is liberating.

Lies bind a person and cause confusion. This is because the person must keep up with the lies that they have told. There is a saying, "The truth will always outrun a lie."

People can change. Only God can change them if they want to change. God does not go against our will. He gives us freedom of choice.

Chapter 5

What Faith Is NOT!

- Faith is not pimping a prophecy gift for the highest dollar.
- Faith is not getting into debt up to your eyeballs and praying for a money miracle.
- Faith is not calling your bank every day to see if a million dollars has been deposited in your account.
- Faith is not gaining 20 or 30 pounds over time and praying for a weight loss miracle.
- Faith is not eating everything in sight then you get diagnosed with a medical condition and you pray for healing.

- Faith is not having a pity party to feel sorry for yourself because things have not worked out as you thought it should.
- Faith is not doing things in your own power with the mindset that God will bless it.
- Faith is not living a lifestyle that is contrary to what the Bible says and expecting to receive the same benefits of the person that is living a holy, sold out to God lifestyle.
- Faith is not a cake walk. There are times that stepping out in faith makes you look to others as if you have loss your mind. If God told you to do it, God will back you up.

There must be an understanding that firstly, you cannot reap what you have not sown. The bible says in Galatians 6:7, "Do not be deceived, God is not mocked [He will not allow Himself to be ridiculed, nor treated with contempt nor allow His precepts to be scornfully set aside]; for whatever a man sows, this *and* this only is what he will reap." (Amplified Version)

A farmer does not sow corn and expect a harvest of peas. This would violate the law of sowing and reaping. Therefore, you cannot sow five dollars and expect a harvest of millions. In addition, there are other factors involved in sowing and reaping such as sowing into good ground. A farmer must break up the fallow ground to make sure it is conducive for sowing seed. It does not do any good to sow seed and you did not sow into good ground.

Second, you must sow your seed with the right spirit or attitude when you give. If not, you missed your blessing in giving your seed. Your seed can be utilized by the ministry it was given to. The bible says, "Let each one give [thoughtfully and with purpose] just as he has decided in his heart, not grudgingly or under compulsion, for God loves a cheerful giver [and delights in the one whose heart is in his gift]." II Corinthians 9:7 Amplified Version Lastly, you must water your seed with expectancy.

While you are waiting for your harvest you water your seed by speaking the word of God over your seed and believing. Before you know it, your harvest will be fully matured and blossom.

You must respect and know the season that you are in. A farmer knows the seasons. Certain seasons are for planting. Another season may be for tilling the ground. Another season is for water the seed and plucking out the weeds. The favorite season of an avid sower is harvest time. Have you sowed to reap a harvest?

Chapter 6

OBEDIENCE!

One key that many overlook is obedience. You must sow what God tells you to sow, when he tells you to sow, where he tells you to sow, and how he tells you to sow. For example, I was listening to the televangelist Creflo Dollar one day. He stated that God spoke to him concerning giving a brother in the church one of his suits in his closet. He gave that brother every suit but the one God told him to give.

Finally, he broken down and gave the suit he was supposed to give. He got mad at God and said, "See I only have a few suits left." God spoke back and said, "If you would have given him the suit that I told you to give him in the first place, none of this would have happened." We try to bargain our way out of obedience.

It does not work. We must obey God and obey him the first time he speaks to be successful. If you really want success, check your level of obedience. Are you willing to look like a fool to obey God? Are you willing to take ridicule from man to obey God? Are you willing to not be liked by others or not be popular to obey God? Are you willing to take your mask off to obey God? Or is it all about appearances? We as believers in Jesus Christ say we don't celebrate Halloween. But we do if we wear a mask all the time and are not transparent with God and ourselves. It's not necessarily about being transparent with man. Man can't help us. It's about being transparent with the maker and creator of our ever-dying soul. There came a time in my walk with God where he posed this question to me, "Do you trust me?" I had to be honest with him and myself. I told the Lord "No." This was a reality check for me. He knew I did not trust him as I should as a believer. I did not know that I did not trust him.

God will shine the light on the secret and subtle things that are hidden, if we allow him. We must allow God to deal with us in totality not just here and there.

Obedience does not just relate to sowing and reaping or money. Obedience relates to all aspects of the Christian lifestyle. There are several examples in the bible. Hebrews 11 talks about the heroes of faith. You have people like Noah, Abraham, and many others. Speaking of Noah, he built an ark out of obedience and instruction from God. The Lord gave him specific instructions. He was instructed on what kind of wood to use and was told the heights and widths for construction of the ark. In Noah's time, it had never rained before. He foretold of the rain that was coming. People thought that Noah was crazy but when the sky became thunderous and the flood waters came, those same people who did not believe were beating on the door to the ark screaming, "Let us in!" It was too late.

The word of God says, "God shut the door." This means that Noah could not open the door to the ark even if he had wanted the door opened. The scripture reference for this bible story is Genesis 6:5 - Genesis 7:24 (KJV).

If you want what someone else has then how about you deeply consider the price that they paid to get it. Many want what others have but do not want to pay the price that they have paid to get it. To walk a serious faith walk comes with a price. As believers, it is imperative that we count the cost to follow Christ. There are many that are going to bow under the pressure of this world. Especially now that the chip technology is slowly being implemented into our society. They say it is for our protection. However true believers know that such is setting the stage for the mark of the beast.

Will you have faith enough not to take the chip when the word of God says without the mark of the beast (the chip) you will not be able to buy or sell? Are your actions of faith? Or are they of ignorance disguised as faith? You be the judge.

Chapter 7

Questions for Self-Reflection

Do you have faith?_____

If yes, what do you have faith in?

_____

_____

_____

Is your faith misplaced? Is it in people or things that can't save your soul?

_____

_____

_____

_____

_____

You have acted in a way that you thought that is was faith but it was not using wisdom?

_____

_____

_____

_____

_____

What were your results?

_____

_____

_____

_____

Positive or negative?

_____

_____

_____

_____

Based on the results, will you operate differently in the future? (Yes or No)

_____

If no, why not?

_____

_____

_____

_____

If yes, How so?

_____

_____

_____

_____

Has this book helped you? Why or why not?

_____

_____

_____

_____

If you are not a believer in Jesus Christ and you would like to accept him as your savior, please say this prayer:

> Father forgive me. I am a sinner. Jesus come into my heart and be the Lord of my life. I will live for you as you show me how. In Jesus name, I pray. Amen

- Romans 10:9 says "That if thou shalt confess with thy mouth the Lord Jesus, and shalt believe in thine heart that God hath raised him from the dead, thou shalt be saved. (KJV)

You have now given your life to Christ find a bible believing church to fellowship with like minded people. You are now on a new journey of faith and a new lifestyle. You just asked Jesus to come into your heart to lead and directed in every decision you make. Do not think it strange the things that will now happen in your life. This is not an easy path however it is a good path. I hope that you have been blessed and enlightened by the words on the pages. The only hope we have is in Christ Jesus.

www.ingramcontent.com/pod-product-compliance
Lightning Source LLC
Chambersburg PA
CBHW031242120626
46545CB00003B/1241